AF485844

From here, I want to express my gratitude to Amazon and the entire KDP team, for the help provided, in the publication of this humble work.

(And also to Google, for its enormous and priceless work of digitizingbooks)

Contact: andoenmanuelgall@gmail.com

The ancient Roman Roads in Hispania.

5

Errors and new locations

Errors and gaps in the Itinerary A. A. et Hierosolymitanum, proposals for the location of mansions and cities, analysis, etc.

Ello is Caudete in Albacete.

Aspis is Elda.

Laminio is Almodovar del Campo.

Titulcia is Illescas.

Tritium is Burgos.

Esuri is Castro Marim

Pace iulia is Castelo Branco

And so on.

(Some keys to better knowledge)

Introduction

When someone starts reading about the subject of the roads, ancient Hispanic highways in times of the Roman Empire, and delves into the Via Augusta, (although the name is very generic) the longest in the Iberian Peninsula, one finds one, with a huge amount of research and data work, which immerse us at the same time: at one end, a microcosm with infinite details, on the one hand, and on the other hand, at an immense distance, with a global vision of the subject of roads in the Roman Empire, but making a leap between cities, colonies *or "mansionis"* (Plural of *mansio*) that are distanced from about 10 km to 90 km.

But there are few works that link and coordinate, a "medium" vision between the very specialized of the universities, and that of the most generalist of the amateurs, who perhaps provide a more global vision and perhaps with more creativity, and more passion, than scientific and documentary rigor.

The union of both seems to be the most fruitful for their knowledge, and for culture in general.

It must be remembered that, in the topics of History, it is necessary to prioritize and highlight, to try to document everything, and with what is not possible, it is necessary tomark that they are opinions of the author, or that the indications "seem" to lead to theories or working hypotheses. It should not be deduced, without a very complete basis, because they will always be personal and very subjective deductions, which will always depend on the knowledge of the author and his method and access to reach the largest number, of data.

Although it is an issue that seems to us almost impossible to achieve, we must try. In Social and Cultural Anthropology, this defect is called: *Ethnocentrism*; and it results from the application of the particular (E inevitable) personal sense or opinion of the author when investigating and drawing conclusions. Which will always tend to be a bit subjective.

This simple and brief work tries to clear paths towards a better understanding of the Roman road called the Via Augusta, (Generic) between the current Cádiz and its route to *Ad Pyreneum*, on the border with present-day France. And by the way, a proposal for the location of Laminio, Ad Ellum, Aspis, Ossio, Tritium, etc., and already put on the subject, the analysis of other roads or routes, and other contributions, or proposals.

He also tries (humbly) to open new avenues of research, which enrich us all, with his safe documentary contributions and extensions of the subject.

Some guidelines, bases, and recommendations.

Where to support our possible studies, their reading, and for a better understanding of the subject, we advise and note and highlight that:

A)-The most reliable documentary bases are almost all based on the so-called <<Itinerary of Antoninus>> and on the << Vicarello Vessels>>. The other documents are written several hundred years after the construction of the roads and can be considered as made or compiled *"By hearsay"*, which loses much of their rigor. Eye, they have their documentary importance, but you have to study and investigate a lot to be able to document correctly.

As it is popularly said: You have to take them with tweezers

But beware, within the different "Itineraries" with the complements of the authors who have expanded or complemented their study, throughout history, we must highlight the work completely:

<<Itinerarium Antonini Augusti Et Hierosolymitanum>>

(Gustav Parthey, author and Moritz as editor, circa 1848)

It's advice, but if you want you can check it out.

Even the Vessels of Vicarello, are "written" molded or engraved around the year 330.

B) -We must bear in mind at all times, the extraordinary quality, professionalism, common sense, continuous technical advances, etc., and in that line of pragmatism, we must value the great search for the practical and functional, in everything that the engineers of the Roman Empire built.

Apart from the artistic vein and aesthetics of each moment or situation. Which can be seen very clearly in the completion of some buildings and constructions.

From the masterful use of dry stone, that is, to build without mortar or cement, or the way to extract gold from the mountains of León, the mastery in making tunnels, the immensity of its pure water pipes to cities such as the 500 km in Byzantium, the masterful and beautiful aqueduct of Segovia, the construction of the roads, etc., etc.

This brief reminder is for the reader to apply to the design, construction, purpose and more, of Roman roads, or "Ways".

C) -Although they do not finish believing it (Investigate) the term *"Puebla"* in Spanish, *Pobla* in Valencian or Catalan, *Pobra* in Galician and Portuguese, means: that it is a **mutatio.**

And although documentarily it cannot be demonstrated due to lack of data or archaeological remains (At the moment), if it can be affirmed that it is, by the position and distance between the *"mansionis"* registered and documented. For example, in the Pobla de Farnals, just halfway between Valencia and Sagunto. Or between Cartagena, (Murcia) and the next *mansio*, Thiar, towards Elche, where La Puebla as a town of Cartagena, is the first *mutatio*. (Expanded later.)

In La Pobla Llarga, in Valencia, the remains of the road pass through the middle of the town. They are visible.

All of Hispania is full of "Pueblas"

D) –The term "Losa" Losilla" and "Albalat", "Albalate", etc., indicate that it is a road, causeway, road, etc.

E)-The Latin term **-ad,** comes to mean, apart from other uses, and in a simplified way, something like: "a", "towards"; and as an example, we have Ad Turres (Towards the Towers), or Ad Statuas (Towards the statues).

Ad Morum = Towards wild morality. (There are several, in Murcia, Jaén, Italy, etc.)

Ad Turres = Towards the towers. Also, throughout the empire.

Ad Statuas = Towards the statues. Several.

Ad Putea = Towards... ¿?

Ad Ellum = Towards the city of Ello (Caudete de Albacete)

Etc.

But that's reducing it very quickly. Because **–ad,** it comes to express a large number of things, such as:

-*Direction* in space, in time and in the affective and moral order. It can also be applied to: **go to, up, against,** etc.

-*Proximity,* adaptation, together with, precise determination of place, etc., etc.

-*Purpose,* destiny, intention, attentive to combat, etc., etc.

-*Relationship,* comparison, opposition, response, conformity, etc.

F) -The Latin term **-Sub,** comes to indicate something like: *under, in view of, at the foot of the mountain,* etc., example in Tarragona, *"Sub saltus"* (In view of the gorge or gorge?)

-Others.

List of the sections that are analyzed.

And map with the Roads analyzed.

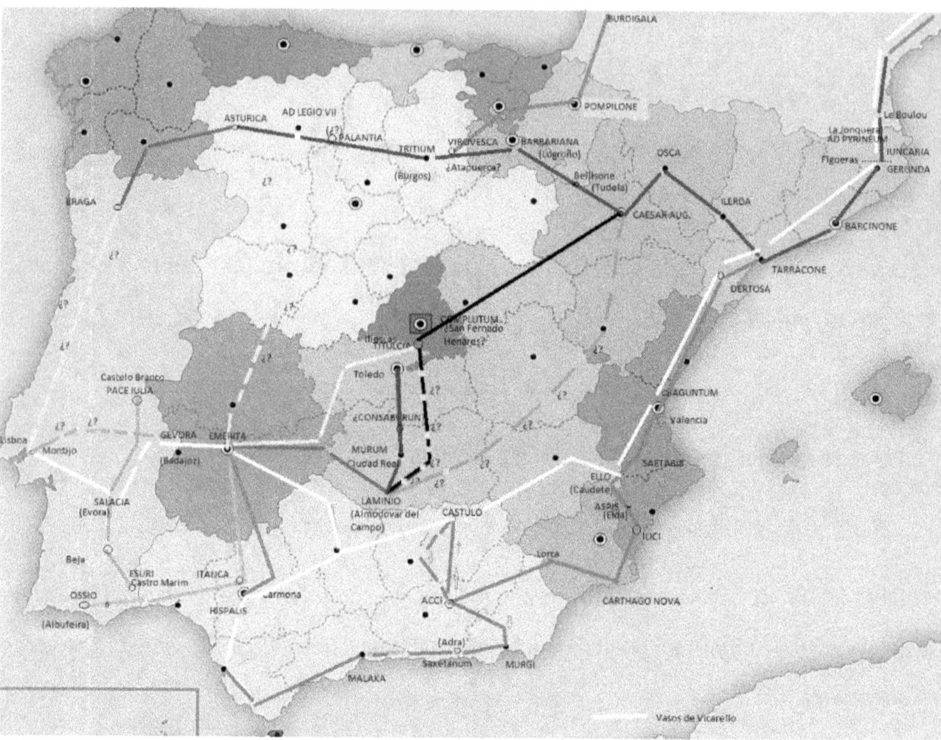

These are some of the 34 Ways, which Saavedra numbered in the nineteenth century, plus 2 that are addedin and numbered as A-22a and A-22b to personalize, define and analyze them as such and their contribution.

(Enlargeor the map, at the end of the book)

Section 0 -Errors, gaps and considerations to be taken into account about the roads or routes that are related in the Itinerary Antonini Augusti et Hierosolymitanum.

(Reading it is almost essential to understand what is proposed next.)

Section 1-This is Caudete, in Albacete, with total security.

-Aspis is Elda, in Alicante, with total security.

-Ilici is Elche in Alicante, with total security.

Section 2-Laminio is Almodóvar del Campo, in Ciudad Real.

Section 3- Titulcia es Illescas. Toletum is Toledo and Complutum may be the current San Fernando de Henares. (Complutum, it is not known with certainty where it was)

- Carthago Nova is Cartagena, in Murcia, with total security.

-From Valentia to Cástulo. (Valencia-Linares)

- Toletum is Toledo, for sure.

- Caesaraugusta is Zaragoza, for sure.

Section 4-The Vessels of Vicarello, document the mansionis from Cádiz to Linares, (Cástulo). And from Cástulo to Ad Aras (Ventas de Fuente la Higuera) and Játiva. Then it continues to Rome, recording a new and particular series of "Stops", Mansionis, or Mutationis, different or absent, to those of the original Itinerary of Antonini Augusti.

Section 5-Saltigi, seems to be around Albacete city.

Section 6- Some errors in the registration of the various "Antonini Augusti Itineraries"

(Analysis of the A-1, A-32 and A-34 route)

Section 7- Libisosa is Lezuza in Albacete?

Section 8-Hispania, was Spain and Portugal

Section 9-Great fans and their contribution.

Section 10- Tolous is Monzón de Huesca.

Section 11- Burgos was the mansio Tritium.

Etc.

"Fools are in a hurry,

where angels are afraid to tread"

John White, in <<The Mystical Experience>>

Beginning

The "Via Augusta" enters or begins in Hispania, coming from Rome, crossing the entire French Mediterranean.

On Spanish soil, the first mansio can be considered as that of Ad Pyreneum, and procomes from the French Ad Stabulum about XVI Roman miles, about: 23.7 km along the current roads, whose layout usually coincides with that of the Roman roads.

The next mansio, towards Girona, is Iuncaria to other XVI mpm. 23.7 km.

And then Gerunda (Girona) follows to XXVII mpm. About 40 km.

And this relationship is according to page 188 of the Itinerarium A. A. et Hyerosolimitanum, by G. Parthey

(Digitized by Google. Thanks a lot. Immense gratitude)

And this clarification is basic, because then on page 191, the same route is reflected, but based on the so-called Vicarello Vessels. Que, in turn, will also change the name or denomination to some mansions of the route.

It seems clear that the traveler who collected the "Stops" or Mansions at that time, in the Vessels of Vicarello, did not know or had lost the names and place names and place names "original" or primitive, of the official Itinerary of the Roman Empire.

Recall, that the hypothesis proposed by this author, previously, is that the Vessels, may have been made around the yearss 330-340.

And the copy of the Itinerary will be made around 330. Shortly after the creation of the city of Constantinople as the new capital of the Roman Empire.

Appearing as a mansio the city of *Constantinopoli,* it seems appropriate to date the copy of the Itinerary around the year 330. (As some author pointed out before).

In the <<Pteungerian Bull>>, ancient map of the Mediterranean, Constantinople also appears. Although the analysis of this map made in the thirteenth century, a mixture of cities appears, some of the Itinerary as main roads and others of secondary roads.

(Conrad Mannert pointed out in the nineteenth century, that Castro Marim was the mansio Esuri, studying the Tabula. Incredible. And, this Castro is located almost opposite the current Ayamonte, but in Portugal)

It also appears as mansio: Eliocroca, the current Lorca in Murcia. And it comes from Carthago Nova, and heads towards Andalusia. If, as proposed in the <<History of the Bishopric of Cartagena>> the Council of Elvira was held in 328, the Itinerary may have taken the data and reflects it towards the year 330.

Well, as it seems that all the researchers of the world, of the subject Roman roads, have made the aforementioned Itinerary, their particular bible, but not reasoning the locations of the mansions, and reaffirming and publishing some errors that I consider bulky, some changes are proposed, always with the humility and the healthy intention of giving a little cultural light on this subject.

The proposal is as follows: from Narbonne in France to Tarragona, and starting with the last French mansio and the first Spanish:

Ad Stabulum is the French: Le Boulou.

Ad Pyreneum is La Jonquera. (XVI miles, 23.7 km from Le Boulou)

Iuncaria is Figueras.   (A XVI mpm of the previous one, 23.7 km by the current roads)

Gerunda is Girona.   (A XXVII mpm of the previous one, 40 km by the current roads)

Barcenone is Barcelona. Here there is no doubt and the mpm and the km by road also coincide.

Towards Tarragona, the mansio appears: Stabulo novo, adding in total: 75 miles. In km there are 111.

This mansio of Stabulo novo disappears in the Vessels of Vicarello and appear in its place, those of Fines, Antistiana and Palfuriana, which add up to 66 mpm. VIIII miles are missing. Why?

Possibly, after the invasion of Franks and Alamanni in 262, the new route of the Via between Barcelona and Tarragona, becomes shorter; perhaps it separates from the coast and takes advantage of another road, narrower, more uncomfortable and of lower category, but necessary for the service.

It remains to be investigated.

Then, from Tarraco, the Vía heads towards Lleida and Zaragoza, on the one hand, and on the other to Valencia and Cartagena.

From Tarraco to Caesaraugusta, the miles coincide fully with the kms, and along the same route as the current great roads. But we must bear in mind that, this section passes through Osca, (Huesca) and between Tarragona and Lleida, the miles do not coincide with the real kilometers between these two capitals.

Also add that the mansio of *Tolous*, XXX miles, 47 km from Lleida towards Huesca, is Monzón in Huesca. As I pointed out on page 393 of Parthey's Itinerary. (In other locations they do not get it right)

Then, this Way continued to: *Ad VII Legio Gémina.* The current Leon, in which everyone agrees.

From Zaragoza, it seems to pass through Calahorra, Logroño, Nájera, crosses the province of Burgos and in an almost straight line, reaches León, where the total of Roman miles, coincide (km up or down) with the km by road.

Paragraph 0

Errors and gaps in the itinerary Antonini Augusti Et Hierosoliymitanum. (Hispania)

This list or compilation of the roads or Roads of the various "Itineraries" of the Roman Empire, was written by Gustav Friedrich Konstantin Parthey, (1798-1872) who was a philologist and art historian, born in Berlin.

(The Itinerary Antonini Augusti Et Hierosolymitanum, published in 1848)

Let us now look at a small list of the locations of mansionis or mutationis on the Roman roads in Hispania in the year 300, in what this humble author considers erroneous, and some gaps in routes, or stretches of roads, which can help to understand the context and circumstances of the author or authors who transcribed the copy of the (Almost certainly) last Antonini Augusti Itinerary. (In alphabetical order)

It must be made very clear that these possible errors or gaps, which are then related and analyzed in a simple way, but I think that forceful, are not Parthey's fault or attributable to his work, since his work is basically a (Very good) work of data collection and opinions and theories of other authors, that sinned of documentary recklessness, and some presumptuous protagonism. That is, unverifiable.

As a "good" German, Gustav Parthey was prudent, and left for others the fantasy, the weak and subjective deductions, and the desire for personal fame of some authors who still today, in the year 2020, market and sell themselves to egocentric whims, and to the: "Anything goes"

From this Itinerary, all the scholars of the world have suckled culture and data since it was published. But the mistakes and gaps have been transmitted all over the world as well. Thus, at the University of Lund, in Sweden, like most of Europe, it is still reflected in the digital, geographical and historical maps, that Elda in Alicante, is the mansio Ad Ellum.

(Gross error. As shown below)

Well, let's also keep in mind that:

The distance between mansionis is divided into equal parts, (almost always), where the mutationis are installed; which are of particular management and size, much smaller, such as the mansionis with many more services and in charge of the Res Pública, that is, depending on the imperial administration.

For example, between Saguntum and Valentia, there is a distance of XVI Roman miles. This route is divided into two pieces of VIII mpm, and the mutatio of Puebla de Farnals appears. (It is a proposal)

Between Ad Ellum (Caudete) and Aspis (Elda) there are XXIIII (24) mpm, which is divided into three sections, of VIII Roman miles each.

In other sections, the distances between mutations may vary, as may be the case proposed: From Carthago Nova to Eliocroca there is XXXXIIII mpm; here the distance between stops can be four to VII mpm, and two to VIII mpm. 28 + 16 = 44 mpm.

(Discussed below)

Well, fromthe literal of parthey's book (Itinerarium), they are awarded:

Ad Ello = Elda in Alicante, according to the researcher (From the nineteenth century) Cortés, Reichard and others. Alforines in Valencia, (according to the "daring") Paul Lapie, which should refer to the current Fontanars dels Alforins (In Valencian), on the road from Fuente la Higuera to Onteniente. Page 298 of the Itinerary.

Arriaca = Guadalajara

Bilbili = Ateca or Calatayud.

Complutum = Alcalá de Henares

Consabro = Consuegra.

Lamini = Wire fence in Ciudad Real (Reichard and Mannert) Daimiel according to Cortés, and Don Sancho, according to Lapie.

Libisosa = Lezuza.

Murum = Morotales (?) Quesada in Jaén (Lapie) or Villarta. (It must refer to Villarta de San Juan, camino de Alambra.)

Parietinis = Chinchilla according to Cortés and San Clemente de Cuenca, according to Lapie.

Saltici = Jonquera in Albacete or Santa Maria del Campo, in Cuenca, (Lapie). Today for the modern "Lapies", it is Chinchilla.

Titulcia = Near Torrejón or Bayonne or Getafe. According to authors.

Vico Cuminario = Ocaña, Bayonne, in Toledo.

This is only a very brief relationship that will be analyzed more deeply, of the roads in Hispania of the third and third century, (4, as it appears in the Itinerary).

Almost all of them seem to be awarded a little lightly, based on the studies or opinions of nineteenth-century authors, who at that time enjoyed a lot of culture, a lot of time, a lot of power and most, of enough means or money. But this enjoyment of life in general, with respect to the majority of the population, was not reflected in prudence, when making historical judgments or adjudications of the ancient towns or cities of Antiquity. In most of the aforementioned they were wrong.

Statistically, they only get about 15% right.

And, among other things, they lacked the immense amount of information and archaeological, historical studies, etc., and the scientific advances that we have today.

By the way, who invented the IV, like four?

(If in the whole Itinerary, in Latin, the four letters are accepted as numbers)

In a section below, other errors and gaps are detailed with more extension and precision.

Paragraph 1

Ello is Caudete in Albacete. **Aspis** is Elda in Alicante. **Ilici** is Elche in Alicante.

Ad Ellum, was located in the "Ventas" of today popularly called as: Cruce de Fuente la Higuera.

(N-330 Madrid-Alicante junction with the N-344 Valencia-Almería, passing through Yecla and Jumilla)

And **This** is Caudete de Albacete. Safely.

There are many other cities, of which it can be said with **total certainty**, that they were the ancient locations of the Roman Empire, for example:

In Hispania: Lisbon (Olisipone), Elche (Ilici), Cartagena (Carthago Nova), Valencia (Valentia), Tarragona (Tarraco), Barcelona (Barcenone), Gerona (Gerunda), Lérida (Ilerda), Huesca (Osca), Pamplona (Pompelum), Zaragoza (Caesaraugusta), Toledo (Toletum), Játiva (Saetabis), Mérida (Emerita Augusta), Astorga (Astúrica), Sevilla (Hispalis), Málaga (Malaka), Cádiz (Gades) etc., etc.

In many others, there are still doubts, or they need some more confirmation. And from here we will affirm that the ancient **Ello is Caudete** with total certainty.

If we start from the totally reliable base, that **Ilici,** was a mansio located at a distance of XXIIII (24) Roman miles or mpm, from the previous mansio, which was Aspis, coming from Saetabis and Valentia, then it turns out that, on the current road, it runs evenly or a short distance from the Vinalopó river, with its valley, is equal to: 35.5 km.

Then, by a simple measurement, and very easy to check online, **Aspis** is the modern **Elda.**

And from Elda backwards, towards Játiva and Valencia, towards the mansio Ad Ellum, there is an equal distance, of XXIIII mpm = 35.5 km.

That coincides exactly with the Ventas del Cruce de Fuente la Higuera and the national road from Madrid to Alicante, two or three km from the ruins of Ello, in Caudete!

Is it that simple?

Check

In addition, at the aforementioned "crossing", there is a passage under the modern highway that comes from Albacete and Madrid, where there are still remains of a road, with the cornerstones of white marble.

This step is called in Caudete and on maps as "Camino viejo de Fuente la Higuera". And in Fuente la Higuera (Valencia) it is called: "Camino viejo de Caudete". It follows the same route and direction, as the 900 meters of Roman road, which have been discovered in Fuente la Higuera, due or thanks to the works of the high-speed train, from Madrid to Valencia, and the invaluable work of a group of historians and archaeologists from the University of Valencia. Thank you a thousand.

Remember that, in the <<*History of the Bishopric of Cartagena*>> it is stated that Caudete was the seat of the *Elotana church,* and was the holder of an episcopal chair, sending bishops or representatives to several Councils of Toledo and others.

The proposal is, that it was destroyed to the foundations, by the Muslim troops of Cordoba, to put peace, and create with tranquility, the current Murcia, as the new capital of the Cora de Tudmir, around the year 725. (It is included in the document for the creation of Murcia capital)

When the Elotano bishopric disappears, it becomes part of the reborn bishopric of Orihuela, created on July 14, 1564, along with the "island" of territory around the great Iberian-Roman town of Castellar de Meca, between Alpera and Ayora, and a summer palace is built in Caudete, with the symbol of the bishop of Orihuela, which can still be contemplated, as a testimony of living history.

It can be advanced, that when the archaeological zone is excavated in depth with the possible ruins of Ello, near the aforementioned episcopal palace, the history will be greatly enriched with the findings that will surely be found.

It is obligatory and necessary, the comment on the current location of Ello, which can be seen on the internet.

Navigating and taking notes, what is perhaps the oldest **recklessness** about the location of Ello appears. In the *Grand Dictionnaire de la Langue Latine,* by N. Thel, published in Paris, in 1929, she is placed in Elda, Alicante.

Thus, studying the <<Digital Atlas of the Roman Empire>> of the Swedish University of Lund, Ello also appears located in Elda.

Also, in several of the advanced and technically spectacular Digital Atlases of the Roman Empire, which can be seen out there, appears the poor Ello, orphaned and changed place, and the now humble Caudete in Albacete, is still waiting for her hidden treasure to be studied a little, and award her the honor that corresponds to her in history.

And meanwhile, mistakes, and the "ball" runs and runs. Meanwhile, the "angels" and the Germans, fear to step on and maintain a discreet and prudent silence.

Paragraph 2

Laminio, its location and possible errors.

Murum is Ciudad Real

Consabro, it is not known

a) In the Via del Itinerario that in Hispania we can identify as A-30, (According to a simple numbering, which Saavedra already made in the nineteenth century) appears:

Item to **Laminio** *Toletum* mpm XCV sic(Total 95 miles, i.e. 140 km)

Murum... mpm XXVII

Consabro.. mpm XXVIII

Toletum.. mpm XLIIII

The proposal is:

Laminio = **Almodóvar del Campo**, Ciudad Real

Murum = Ciudad Real, capital.

Consabro = In the middle of the road, or current road from Toledo to Ciudad Real. At the same "height" on the maps, as Consuegra. Near the Convent of Santa María del Monte.

The km along the national road from Toledo to Ciudad Real and then to Puertollano or Almodóvar del Campo, coincide completely.

Laminio could also be identified with the old town of "Puerto Plano" (whichseems to be around 1550, as Portus Planus), since the km from Toledo are practically the same to Almodóvar, as to the current Puertollano.

But even though modern Puertollano is bigger, more famous and richer, Almodóvar del Campo has much greater historical, architectural and archaeological heritage. And the endorsement, that the remains of a Roman road (300 by 3.2 meters) between Chillón and the world famous for mercury, Almadén, go to Almodóvar.

Faced with logical doubts or skepticism, we are going to apply another component or variable, or data, and analyze the Way from Mérida to Zaragoza, through Lusitania:

Subparagraph (b)

Per Lusitaniam ab Emerita Caesaraugustam   mpm CCCCLVIII (458), 678 km

Contosolia.. mpm X   II

Mirobriga.. pmp   XXXVI

Sisalone.   mpm XIII

Careuvium.. mpm XX

Ad Turres.. mpm XXVI

Mariana . . mpm XXIIII

Lamini   mpm XXX

And so, on

That is: from Mérida to (Lamini) Almodóvar del Campo: 161miles = **238.44** km

It is difficult or almost impossible to specify the exact route followed by the original road, since the entire area of Extremadura is flooded by the waters of the Guadiana and many of its afluentes, in the Almaraz dam; but by any of the **three** roads with more possibilities, the distance is **237** km!

There is a stretch of road, from Mérida, (La mitad, more or less) that is common to Toledo, Córdoba and Laminio, but then three possible routes or itineraries can be studied or evaluated, with the same kilometers or very similar.

On such a long journey, the distance of a kilometer or two is negligible.

c)   Some authors value and publish in their research the small archaeological remains and other findings, but here it will also be valued, the importance of Almodóvar del Campo or Laminio, as **a world center**, producer and regulator of the most appreciated and more expensive (at that time) than gold: mercury.

Whose fame reached China, and whose use was totally regulated by the Res Pública, the official Administration, of the Roman Empire, which prohibited its direct treatment. So, the cinnabar from which the "azogue" or "vermilion" is extracted had to be sent to Rome for refining.

This seems to be the gift or treasure, which had the disappeared Laminio, to be the head of exit of three roads of the first order in the Empire. Its strategic place, as an outlet of the mineral associated with mercury and its also not inconsiderable contribution such as silver, and some copper. In addition to being strategically located in the natural corridor that communicated Extremadura with the plains of La Mancha.

Other authors compare the imperial mercury trade of the *Ager Laminitanus*, with the wealth of Alhambra, a small town of Ciudad Real and its quarries of sharpening stone!

Is one mining wealth comparable to the other?

Any salt flat of the empire would produce more wealth than the stones of the Alhambra.

Or is it that, as he quotes (and puts it) on page 350 of G.' s Antonini Augusti Itinerary. Parthey, you had to give Alhambra all the credit in the world?

And humility and documentary prudence?

Another of the "graces" or virtues, which can endorse Almodóvar as the rich and important Laminio, (although relatively), is to appear in its municipal area, some epigraphic remains, found in the place of La Bienvenida, road cm-402, where the famous Sisapone is cited, named by Pliny, Strabo, Cicero, etc.

Miguel de Cervantes (Don Quixote) also quotes Almodóvar four times.

It also has in its surroundings, coal mines, Chalcolithic remains, bronze Age, Bronze Argaric sword, Oretan and Roman remains, Visigothic necropolis, etc.

Among other virtues.

As the starting head, there are three, the roads that started from Laminio:

One,   << *Item Laminio to Toletum*>> (Already analyzed before)

Two,   <<*Item a Laminio **alio itinere** Caesaraugusta*>>

(*alio itinere* means: another way, or alternative way)

And the third **that does not appear** anywhere, and that should be the "normal", the first, the direct, the optimized, etc., and that should put:

<<Item to Laminio Caesaraugusta>>

Why is this road not reflected?

It remains to be investigated. Surely there are many miliaries and many hidden "treasures", which will reveal great stories.

Laminius,surely, was greatly affected by the invasion of the Franks and Alamanni around the year 262. And maybe then for the same, in 270.

If these invasions made cities like Ilici disappear, today's Elche and many others, a mining area like Almadén and Almodóvar del Campo, where most of the hard work would be done by slaves, the trade would practically be nipped in the bud.

Normally, the extraction of cinnabar with its mercury and other metals, stopped suddenly, and itstools, its collaborating and cargo animals, and its commercialization also slowed down and reached minimum exploitation, perhaps by local landowners or pure artisanal subsistence.

With the invasions, life throughout Hispania becomes more rural and agricultural, the inhabitants of the towns and cities take refuge in the mountains and in those safer fields or agricultural exploitation furthest from the roads or roads, where the dangerous invaders could return; trade and export are limited to a minimum. With the Roman Peace gone, and trade practically paralyzed, cities are ruined and become dangerous. The crisis is total, added to the civil war in the capital of the empire.

Most of the towns of Hispania are surely abandoned or disappear for decades due to the invasions of the Franks. Then will come those of the Swabians, Vandals and Alans. And then the Goths.

Roads that were not well built or without proper maintenance, disappear in about thirty or forty years.

The first thing is survival, then there will be time for production and luxuries.

(Pending study)

d) In this mentioned road, of section b), from Mérida to Zaragoza, (Per Lusitaniam) a total distance in Roman miles of:

CCCCLVIII = 458, equivalent to **678** kms, on current roads.

If from Emérita to Laminio there are 161mpm = 238 km.

From Laminio to Titulcia there are 82 mpm = 121 km.

And from Titulcia to:

"Caesaraugusta"mansionibus supra scripti" CCXV, 215 mpm = 318 km.

It turns out, they add up to 458 miles, = **777** km.

777 minus the 678 above = 99 km missing.

In this way, if from Laminio to Titulcia (Illescas, in Toledo) there are 99 km left, the conclusion that can be drawn is that the layout of this stretch of road seems impossible to find out.

Several authors, since the nineteenth century, have tried to square the distance from Laminio, although placing it in Alhambra (Ciudad Real) admitting that kms are missing, and mansionis, to the "unknown" Titulcia, and that the most prudent author, Hubnerla situates: *"East of Toledo"*.

(What a good temper the Germans have)

It is one of the lagoons, in the Itinerary, as well as in the road from Cartago Spartaria to Cástulo. On the stretch from Eliocroca to Baza, with only one mansio: Ad Morum.

(e) Another proposed error which also appears or makes the route of the A-31 road seem or appear unsolvable, the so-called:

<<Item a Laminio alio itinere Caesaraugusta>>

The compilation that appears in the Itinerary is as follows:

(Total)   mpm CCXLVIIII sic, =249 miles, 370 km.

Caput fluminis Anae	mpm VII, ... It's, mutate.
Libisosia	mpm XIIII
Parietinis	mpn XXII
Saltici	mpm XVI
Ad Putea	mpm XXXII
Valeponga	mpm XL, En llano
Urbiaca	mpm XX
Albónica	mpm XXV
Agiria	mpm VI ... (It's a mutatium)
Carae	mpm X .... (Mutatio)
Sermon	mpm XXVIIII
Caesaraugusta	mpm XXVIII

The analysis:

The first mansio, that of *Caput fluminis Anae,* is of really ambiguous and insecure localization and translation. Caput, in classical Latin can only be understood by the author who awarded it, but by the distance, from Laminio (Almodóvar del Campo) it can coincide with a place, near: three lagoons that there are currently, that of the Lomillos, the Acebuche and Carboneras. And taking into account the variable, that two thousand years ago, these gaps could be larger. It is a proposal.

According to other authors, in Latin, *the "Caput fluminis Anae"* to be in Accusative could mean:

"Where a road to the Anas River would depart"

Another possible mistake is that the following three mansionis that follow that of Caput: Libisosia, Parietinis and Saltici, (Saltigi) are taken, taken or added from the Vessels of Vicarello.

The so-called Vessels of Vicarello, collect a list of mansionis from Gades (Cadiz) to Rome, but very particular or very personalized. Possibly, these new "stops" or mansionis, are fully updated in their time or historical moment, (Around the year 330) which would support the theory that the invasion of the Franks and Alamanni was much more devastating for Hispania, than what is known until now.

It looks like a "cut and copy" of today. Since then follow the "Stops" towards Játiva, with a typical and unique denomination of the Vessels. Where Ad Turres and Ad Statuas also "disappear".

Perhaps Parthey collected them and introduced them into the Itinerary, but it looks like a filler, or a mistake.

These mansionis could be accepted, if it were not for the fact that there is another discordance or error, and that is that: from the hypothesis that almost everyone accepts and some authors assure that Saltici or Saltigi is the current Chinchilla, up to Zaragoza there is a distance of **395** km.

And we have seen before, how the total from Laminio to Caesaraugusta was **370** km.

It is evident that the distance from Laminio to Saltici is missing. (Many kilometers)

This is another mistake, which also makes it impossible to theorize even on an acceptable basis, about the layout of this road.

Although if one were Roman, the normal thing to not coincide with other routes would be to cross La Mancha towards Valeria, more or less, and continue through Cañete, or Landete in Cuenca, towards Teruel and then to Zaragoza.

It is only a hypothesis, but it is another transport and communication option, between the busy and super famous roads from Mérida to Zaragoza through Toledo, Madrid and Guadalajara, and the old one in the south, from the rich Cástulo (Linares) to Albacete, Játiva, Valencia, Tarragona and the Pyrenees to Rome.

And many others who departed from the capital of Lusitania, such as Emerita Augusta.

And another endorsement, for Laminio to be Almodóvar del Campo, and although recognizing that his contribution is variable and relative and difficult to assess, since it could be considered from a total certificate, to a simple historical or geographical anecdote, let's see and know the following route, which appears in a part of the work:

<<Scophantic Epitame, in which it is about all the cities of the world ... and of all the rules contained in the art of geometry.>>
(Gabriel de Souza Brito)

And titled the section, as "Rotero de España", in which appear around 1706, the list of royal roads of Spain, and that can be considered as the "roads" of the time. Although much poorer and neglected than the Hispano-Roman roads.

It must be taken into account, apart from many other elements, that these roads were almost **all dirt,** except for the sections that took advantage of the roads, which the name of the modern mansionis or mutationis are that of: Ventas, and logically they are all already registered in Spanish, or in local or regional languages.

(As an example, around 1930, from Murcia capital to Cartagena and its important sea port, the road was still dirt)

Well, onpage 483 of this Epitome, (La 512 in pdf) the route appears:

"From Toledo to Cordoua, 49 leagues"

The sales of Diezma	2 and a half
Orgaz	2 and a half
Yevenes	1 (league)
The sale of Guadalherse	2
The sale Daraçutan	2
La Zarçuela	1
Malagón	2
Peralvillo	2
Ciudad Real	2
Caracuel	3
Almodóvar del Campo	3

From here to Córdoba, almost everything is "ventas" (19), except *Damaz* (Adamuz) and *"La puente de Alcolea"*, as the bridges were then called. The Alcolea Bridge is still called that today.

It can be easily appreciated, that after about 1500 years, the shortest and "natural" route from Toledo to Laminio, and then to Córdoba is maintained.

The distances in leagues, suppose an idea, but unreliable, since Spain is still behind in terms of topographic or mathematical culture. The league does not have a fixed measurement, as it can vary from one region to another.

The importance of Laminio or Almodóvar is still important in the eighteenth century and beyond. Mercury production remained a star of the Spanish economy until a few decades ago.

Paragraph 3

Titulcia is Illescas, in Toledo

Titulcia appears as a discreet mansio of the roads, through the center of Roman Hispania, but if we look at its situation a little more carefully, it turns out that it may be the one that is most named, or appears in the different (34) Ways that crossed the Hispania of the Romans.

Like other locations, it seems that only the Itinerary of G. Parthey existed as a reference, in the nineteenth century, or that it really had dazzled the researchers of that time, since on its page 392, it appears "located" in "prope Torrejón" according to Mannert, in Getafe according to Paul Lapie, or in Bayonne according to Cortes, (Ermita de la Bayona, in El Carpio de Tajo?)

Here it is proposed that it is ILLESCAS, in Toledo.

Based on the Via, accepted as A-25, and denominated as:

Appears: Toletum --Titulciam XXIIII mpm

That is, 35.5 km away

If we apply this distance of 35.5 km on the straight, to the road from Toledo to the center (More or less) of Madrid, Illescas appears. On maps, almost total rectilinear appears.

In a super straight line are 33 km, and by road 38.

If we take the mean of these two measures, 33 + 38: 2 = 35.5.

It is too much coincidence, it is fair to recognize it, but as a historical reference and geographical location, it also has its foundation. In addition, it is the third municipality of the province and preserves Romanesque church, and more, that is, it preserves the heritage and prestancia of having been something great and important for centuries.

The next mansio is Complutum, at XXX miles, which are about 44.4 km, and the personal opinion is that, the aforementioned road deviates or also comes from Segovia and Astúrica, and what was said at the beginning of this work is applicable: the quality and tremendous practicality of Roman constructions. That is, from Illescas towards the center of Madrid, the road to the Navacerrada mountain pass approaches and towards the plateau of Castilla León.

And the road will cross the Manzanares and Jarama rivers, avoiding the Guadarrama river on the left and the Tajuña, Henares and Tajo rivers, on the right, and on the upper part, with the softest fords and perhaps easier to cross the banks and with relatively little water flow, where crossing them will not need large stone bridges, and possible damage from rainy winters, or storms, can be repaired in a reasonable and reasonably short time.

If we apply the XXX mpm and its equivalents 44.4 km, from Illescas, the distance will take us to San Fernando de Henares, about twelve or fifteen kilometers before the "awarded" without much base, Alcalá de Henares.

To refute this proposal, among others, you can fall into the temptation of measuring the 35.5 km in a straight line to Alcalá de Henares, and would give us or mark another location, which would also be somewhat short. We have carried out this exercise or temptation, but we are much more convinced by the design, construction and conservation of Roman roads, than the disastrous roads or better would be to say: roads, of eighteenth-century Spain.

Some more notes about our proposal and citing the "Rotero de España" which is a section within the work "Epitome Cosmographico" of the year 1706, are:

From Toledo to Zaragoza, 63 leagues.

Mocejon

Villa Seca

Lorot

Seseña

One Hundred Pozuelos

Lueches

Alcalá de Henares

Etc.

Etc.

The author of this work is the Portuguese Gabriel de Souza, in the service of the King of Spain.

It has already been commented that the leagues of that time do not have a fixed measure. In each region of Spain, it can vary from about 4500 meters to 5500. Incredible.

Analyzing another of the paths that appear in the "Rotero":

On the way from Valencia to Seville, 104 leagues.

Catarroja one league

Chair one league

Mulates a league

Algemesin two leagues

Alcira

La Puebla

Xativa

Etc

Etc

And then on the route of:

Valencia for Granada 75 leagues. Which shares with the previous more than the first 80 km, slightly different measures appear:

Cataroja 1 and a half, leagues**

Alginete 1 medium, leagues**

Alcudia 1 league

Alcoçer

Xativa

Etc.

Comment: It is the same section, but with different measures and stops. All peoples exist today, but it seems that, to be an "official" guide to eighteenth-century Spain, it lacks rigor, or homogeneity in the relationship.

From Alicante to Toledo, the route deviates and shortens, from Villena to Yecla, Jumilla, Pétrola, etc., and does not pass through, Albacete capital.

Etc.

The lack of documents and abandonment, in Hispania and in the period from the year 400 to 1600, seems to have left the roads and routes between the most important cities, to the free and popular development of them. That is, to the wisdom and the most immediate and primary needs of the peoples and their peoples.

(At a popular level it is said that to mark the roads: "The donkey was released with its load and wherever it went, it was the best way")

In this way, with practically no maintenance costs, the roads are marked almost in a straight line, and / or with the slopes as smooth as possible. So that the carts with their load can overcome the slopes.

The backwardness and inculture as a country, seemed evident by the state of its roads, and its records, but it is also something sad that in the XXI century, there are still authors who, in historical questions, affirm, deduce, categorize or dictate, with phrases such as:

"Undoubtedly", "conclusively", etc., etc., when awarding locations.

Suffering from the same lack of documentary basis as in the eighteenth century, and nineteenth and twentieth.

Paragraph 4

Other errors or gaps in the Itinerary

Apart from those indicated in the previous chapter and in section zero, there is another gap, which has been studied by almost all researchers on the subject roman roads.

According to the Itinerary, (from Cartagena to Baza and Guadix,) appears the section from Eliocroca to Basti, in Granada, where only one mansio appears: Ad Morum, to XXIIII mpm (24 miles) of Lorca then appears Baza (Basti) to XVI mpm (16 miles).

Eliocroca--Ad Morum--Basti

In total: from Eliocroca to Basti: 40 Roman miles, multiplied by 1,481mt each mile = 59.24 kilometers.

Today, between Lorca and Baza, there is a distance of around 110 km. By roads, which practically follow the same route that was made in Roman times.

So, something is "missing" in about 50km!

Possibly, only an intermediate mansio is missing, something like about 34 Roman miles (mpm)

A large gap in the record of the Itinerary, which supports the theory that it was done with oral transmission data, a little hearsay. And it is normal, in the opinion of this author and in the application of the devastating invasions of Franks and Alamanni of the year 262 and later in 270. Since the area between Lorca and Granada, would be deserted and abandoned. If today, the feeling of desert and solitude is palpable for many kilometers, it is easy to imagine what could have been two thousand years ago.

It should be remembered that there are records from 1860, in which travelers who arrived in Lorca from Murcia in horse-drawn carriages, and wanted to continue on their way to Andalusia, were reminded that they should "look for life" and follow the path as well as they could.

Today, it is still an arid and long road, absent of villages and villages, for many kilometers.

The proposal on the mansio or mutatio of Ad Morum (Towards the wild morality) is that, the "advisor" of the copyist was confused with the Sale of the Moral that already appears in the maps and records of roads of Felipe II, towards the 1600, on the way from Valencia to Granada. The straightest road, and that passes through Fuente La Higuera-Caudete-Yecla-Calasparra-Caravaca-Archivel-Venta **del** Moral-Puebla de Don Fadrique-Galera (Antigua Tutugi) and Baza.

It should also be borne in mind that the section of the old Itinerary, from Ad Ellum (Caudete) as the main road and with imperial management, does not continue towards Almansa and Albacete, but goes down towards the Mediterranean to Elche and from here to Cartago Nova, and Cástulo.

(It is possible that this route was one of the first and oldest, and from the first-second century, the road, which was of second category, ascended to Imperial Management and with the Vessels of Vicarello the mansionis are officially, registered.)

The reasons are unknown, and it is a possibility that this road from the Pyrenees to Cádiz, passing through the rich Cartagena and then to the richest still Castulo (Linares) going down then to Almeria, Malaga and Cádiz, was the first or most important in Hispania, already designed and used by the Carthaginians.

(Remains to be investigated)

Another topic to study is:

The stretch from Linares (Cástulo) to Játiva (Saetabis) is recorded by the so-called Vessels of Vicarello. Possibly these were some offerings of some wealthy character who traveled from the current Cádiz to Rome. And he must have known of the importance of his offering, perhaps he knew of the disappearances or burning of official records, of the invasions of the Franks, of the transfer of the capital of the empire to Constantinople and of the disasters of the civil wars in Rome and the invasions of the different "barbarian" peoples.

In essence: the "stops" of Ad Statuas and Ad Turres disappear, and those of Saetabis and Ad Aras appear.

Which are discussed below. And where there are also some km of section missing.

Paragraph 5

Tritium is Burgos, Palantia is not known where it is located.

The analysis of the A-32 Route, and its comparison with the A-34.

And these with the A-1

The **A-32** road is called as:

Item ab Astúrica Tarracone, mpm CCCCLXXXII, sic

(That is: From Astorga to Tarragona, 482 Roman miles)

And the mansionis are:

Fence   mpm XVI

Interamnio   mpm XIII

Pallantia   mpm XIIII

Vimination   mpm XXXI

Lacobriga   mpm X * (On the A-34, XV appear)

Dessobriga   mpm XV

Segisamone   mpm XV

Deobrigula   mpm XV

Tritium   mpm XXI

Etc.

(It continues to Zaragoza and ends in Tarragona.)

a)-Well, this first section, from Astúrica to Tritium, adds up to 150 Roman miles, which, multiplied by 1,481 meters of a mile, is equal to **222** kms.

(Recall that a Roman mile, mpm, en Latin: *mille passus*, plural: *milia passuum*, it is accepted that it is 1481 meters away. Based on the passage of a Roman legionary, since it advances the left foot and ends with the right, which are about 1,481mts.)

The distance from Astorga to Burgos, on the national road N-120 (Astorga to Logroño), and passing through León, is **224!**

In a straight line they are 195 mt, and for some detours 216 km.

With the statistical bias that can be applied to the distances cited, and other possible variables, it is impossible not to fall into the joy of placing Tritium as the current Burgos.

b)- From Tritio (Burgos), the next mansio, which is Virovesca, the road deviates towards Pamplona and Burdigala, current Bordeaux in France. And on the other hand, take the course to Zaragoza and Tarragona.

Now let's see and analyze the possible "errata", "errors" or gaps, which appear on the A-34 road:

(In short, from Astorga in León, to Bordeaux, in France)

Mansionis common to the a-32 appear. As they are:

Fence   mpm XVI

Interamnio   mpm XIII

Palantia   mpm XIIII

Vimination   mpm XXXI

Lacobrigam   mpm XV *

(Dessobriga does not appear)

Segisamone   mpm XV

Deobrigula   mpm XV

Tritium   mpm XXI

Virovesca   mpm XI From this mansio, the road continued towards Pamplona and Bordeaux. (And also, to Zaragoza)

The errors marked with an asterisk and commented very succinctly, logically vary the partial distances, but it is seen that the global distance does coincide.

These errors that have been marked in smaller print, seem to be errata or small failures of the author, or the printer, totally excusable, but they are examples of what can happen on other roads. As in the section from the Pyrenees to Caudete, or the section from Eliocroca (Lorca) to Baza in Granada.

Or in the great mix of mansionis, from Gades to Ad Aras, which is located in Fuente la Higuera in Valencia. (It's another localization proposal)

It was already commented that the Vessels of Vicarello would be made in late times with respect to the first design of the Itineraries. Almost certainly around the year 340.

They are discussed below.

To complicate matters a little more, let's analyze the **A-1**, regarding its comparison with the previous A-32 and A-34.

The A-1 comes from Italy, passes through Narbonne in France and enters Hispania through the mansio Ad Pirineum, which as another author pointed out, we agree that it is the current one: **La Junquera.**

Without a doubt and very easily demonstrable. Discussed below.

From La Junquera it continues to Girona, Barcelona and Tarragona. From the old Tarraco turn towards Ilerda (Lleida), Osca (Huesca) and go down to Caesaraugusta (Zaragoza).

From Zaragoza to Burgos through Logroño and Santo Domingo de la Calzada are recorded: 125 mpm = 185 km.

From Burgos to León: 175 mpm = 259 km, more or less.

185 km, plus 259 km = **444** km

On current roads: **455 km.**

The itinerary coincides, but the mansionis give rise to confusion and pending issues to investigate, for the following:

--Why does the A-1 reach León and not Astorga?

If from Astorga they depart or arrive: towards Braga in Portugal, towards Bordeaux in France, to Tarragona, another alternative road to Braga, another road along the coast from Braga, another *Item to Bracara Asturicam* (With mansionis different from the first), to Zaragoza by Cantabria, (A-27).

(A-19, A-20, A-21, A-22 and A-27)

In this case it's all guesswork. And more study.

Perhaps, with the passing of the years and the different avatars, invasions, civil wars, etc., that Hispania suffers, the former mansio called: *Ad Legio VII Gemina,* becomes more important. Perhaps, the barracks of a legion, better withstood the onslaught of invasions and wars, to the detriment of the rich and commercial Astúrica, which seems to have been left out and somewhat isolated from the old commercial circuits.

The crisis of the empire of the third century, with the numerous assassinations of emperors, should not have benefited the official records of the Administration.

Note. The city of León, does not take the name from the Latin "Legio", but is renamed by the Franco-Castilian conquerors in its expansion during the so-called "Reconquista", around the year 1017, when it receives the Fuero de León, which was a series of advantages and perks to be able to develop as a city. The name comes from France and from <<Léon>> a saint. Consult the work:

<<Male France and Grandma Germany.

Origin of place names and surnames from all over Spain and Portugal>>

(Ando-Enmanuel Gall.)

On the A-1, the following mansions appear in the section Ad Legio VII Gemina--Tritio, (León a Burgos):

Ad Legio VII Gemina

Lance	mpm VIII
Camala	mpm XXVIIII
Lacobriga	mpm XXX
Segesamone	mpm XLVII
Verovesca	mpm XI**
Segasamunclo	mpm XVIII**
Libya	mpm XVIII**
Tritium	mpm XVIII

(Remember, we have discovered that Tritium is Burgos, and we will start from this basis for later studies)

And analyzing the **A-32**, we see that from Burgos (Tritio) to Zaragoza the mansionis appear:

Virovesca	mpm XVI**
Atiliana	mpm XXX
Barbariana	mpm XXXII
Gracuris	mpm XXXII
Bellisone	mpm XXVIII
Caesaraugusta	mpm XXXVI

a-   On this road (A-32) it appears with **-i,** Virovesca.

b- And in the direction from Tritium to Caesaraugusta. (Burgos to Zaragoza)

c- On the A-1, it appears as Verovesca and from Tritium to Ad legio VII Gemina. That is, on the other side of Tritum (Burgos)

d- The sum of miles from León to Burgos (Ad Legio VII-Tritium) is 185 mpm, which is equivalent to 273 km.

e- The actual distance on the N120 is 173 km. Then, there are about a hundred kilometers left.

f- **It seems** then, that there are plenty of three mansionis: Verovesca, Segasamunclo and Libya, towards Tritium.

g)- As simple and misguided homonymy (with how dangerous it is) in Wikipedia virovesca is related to what is the current Briviesca, in Burgos.

Or someone has "uploaded" it to the Net, taking it from page 399 of the aforementioned Itinerary of Gustav Parthey, without any documentary reference or mention of author.

(Admittedly, the Wiki contemplates it in the state of: "Discussion." It is prudent)

But with the fame it has as a center of consultation worldwide, Wikipedia is inducing a mistake in Everyone!

If this author is right, and Burgos is Tritio, and Briviesca is at a distance of 44 km from Burgos, and the mansio of Virovesca is located at mpm XVI, which is 23.3 km., it seems clear that:

Virovesca, is NOT Briviesca.

By the distance translated into kilometers, Virovesca would be by the town of Atapuerca, moreor less. Within a radius of 23 km, starting from the center of the capital of Burgos.

A proposal that can have many possibilities, is the one that is located in the town of Villamórico, 22.4 km, from Burgos, on the N-120, which comes from León and from Burgos follows Santo Domingo de la **Calzada,** Logroño, Tudela and Zaragoza.

And from here, we propose, place and adjudicate:

Barbariana = Logroño

Gracurris = Calahorra

Bellisone =Tudela

The distances in km, are almost exact, and agree with their equivalent in miles of the Itinerary, (mpm)

Paragraph 6:

Mutations from Cartagena to Lorca

When the so-called Via Augusta, which comes from Rome to the Phoenician Qartadahast (or Cartago Nova in Latin, after the conquest by the Romans) and then continues to the very rich Cástulo (Linares in Jaén), it seems that it already had a precedent as a path in the tradition of African Carthage, and in turn, in the great Persian empire of King Darius I, that in the fifth century BC.C., ordered the construction of a road of almost 2700 km, from Susa, near the Persian Gulf, to the Mediterranean in the city of Sardis, almost neighboring Ephesus.

This brief introduction is to remember that the roads were built with a clear military, controlling and commercial plundering purpose. Apart logically, from its clear postal service, etc., etc.

It is also proposed, to this Hispanic way, as it is one of the oldest designs, for the mining extraction of the area made by the Carthaginians, Greeks and of course the Indigenous Iberians, Massienos, or Contestanos. That is, the different tribes or clans that lived before the Greeks arrived or perhaps, the Egyptians.

The golden age of this area can be located from the third century a.C. to the year 50 of our Era, more or less. So, Cartago Nova, is a very important goal on the Via Augusta, for its mining wealth, sea port, fish production, shopping and rest center, etc.

Let's make a point and remember, the three categories or types of roads or roads, which were in the Roman Empire:

The *viae publicae,* were the most important and had an average width of six to twelve meters. Apart from being better built, their maintenance was in charge of the Empire, so after the invasions of Franks and Alamanni of the year 262, it is almost certain that no one repairs them.

The *viae vicinales,* start from the previous ones and used to unite several villages. They were the most numerous and their width was 3.2 to 6 meters.

The viae privatae, unían the main properties, the *villae*, with the *viae vicinales* and *publicae*. They were private, reserved for the exclusive use of the owner who financed it in its entirety.

The average width of a *private road* was 2.50 to 4 m.

The great roads or public, started from the Forum, so it is possible that in Cartagena, the road entered through the Byzantine gates arranged by Comenciolo, Subida de San Diego and ended in the Plaza de San Francisco.

(In Valencia, the forum was located in the Plaza de la Virgen. So, the Way would enter on one side and exit on the other)

The proposal is as follows:

All the authors, point out and mark, with great security, the exit of the city to Lorca, by the current "Gates of Murcia", when the most appropriate according to the pragmatic Roman philosophy, (commented above) is that the starting point is the door of the city of "all life", near the old Plaza de Bastarreche, and where a piece of Byzantine wall is preserved.

City reinforced and documented by the Byzantine governor (magister militum), Comenciolo around the year 589, who had a marble plaque commemorating the event engraved.

This door directly received visitors from Elche (Ilici), and Thiar, who used the Via or road, with the category of state, imperial, or first order.

And with this assignment, the mansio of Carthago Nova, had to have complete services regarding the attention and needs of the troops, their horses, implements, etc.

From Alicante, the mansio before Cartagena was that of Thiar, municipality of Orihuela, documented by the technicians of its City Council, although today it is a private property and located near Campoamor.

From Thiar, whose name, according to nineteenth-century scholars, is of Phoenician origin, (Ending in -ar) you can draw a totally rectilinear line to Cartagena and to the Plaza de la Estación, of the train, and coincides almost entirely with a current road. (See some map)

The proposed route is, with very slight variations:

Thiar----13km---Pozo Aledo-----13km-----La Puebla-----13km----Cartagena

Being La Puebla and Pozo Aledo, the intermediate mutations.

What is not at all clear, is to locate with some accuracy, the exact point of the exit of a road and its point of arrival. In large or medium-sized cities, it had to be the forum from which the zero km would be marked, that is: the zero Roman mile. But in small villages (Vicus) they would deviate along the route most convenient to their maintenance and durability. Or they would be kept a little away, according to the oldest design, as for example in Játiva, Caudete (Ad Ellum), and others.

All these points would be marked with the miliaries, where they were reflected carved in low relief, as many data as possible.

While these points are located, in this section from Carthago Nova, the **point of arrival** from Alicante, in which the legionaries, with their centurions and chiefs, plus their auxiliaries, women, war apparatuses, etc., etc., could be located on the plain of the Renfe train station, just about 300 meters from the main gate of the city of Cartagena.

(They are calculated, about two auxiliaries, for every ten legionaries)

A legion of between 4500-5000 soldiers, with their companions, does not fit in a city so limited in its surface and its services. It seems more appropriate, that the camp or building of the services of the mansio, was located in the aforementioned Station, with sufficient extension to house what was needed. It's just an idea.

The main exit of Cartagena, is the same as the entrance, the gates of Comenciolo. (The highest part of "Subida San Diego" Street).

And the conviction of this idea, is the logic and practicality of the Romans, which was commented on above. And now another alternative is proposed.

All the authors who deal with the subject, take for granted and affirm without any reluctance, that he left Carthago Nova by the now called Doors of Murcia. And all point out, that from these Doors came from the "pull" to Eliocroca (Lorca), or to Complutun.

The trip to Lorca was, with irony, like a teleportation.

The Causeway to Complutum, it is seen, which is a second-order road, so it only appears in the work of the Anonymous of Ravenna, written apparently around the year 670 and with older documents. But the experts' analysis points out that it is a bit ambiguous and sometimes exorbitant.

Complutum is placed by all the authors in Alcalá de Henares, but here in this work, it is proposed that it be closer to Madrid capital, by San Fernando de Henares.

But as in the Hierosolymitanum, he says that Complutum is in Alcalá de Henares, because Olé! everything is already said!

This mentioned output has several drawbacks and are all geographical in nature. The first barrier is that of the water of the so-called Mandarache Sea, which has been maintained, although alternately, for centuries, and practically to this day. Later it was called El Almarjal, and today it is completely covered with asphalt and buildings.

This "sea" received almost all the rainfall that the Rambla de Benipila collected, from two slopes; one, the one that comes from the rambla from the town of Perín and that reaches the back of the Peñas Blancas. About 15 kilometers long picking up the storms, which every ten years or so, continue to cause flooding.

On the other hand, the waters from the rambla that comes from Pozo los Palos, La Aljorra and surrounding areas were also collected.

The first detour from the Rambla de Benipila, was made in the eighteenth century, when the Arsenal of the Navy was fortified and walled. So, leaving Cartagena and having to cross a bridge, which would surely destroy every ten years, floods, was not the philosophy of the Roman Empire.

But it is that, a few kilometers later, by the slope of Los Ladrillares, they would cross the same rambla again. In short, this section and exit is full of geographical features that need many bridges.

While by the entrance of Comenciolo, which comes from Elche, it borders El Almarjal, or Mar de Mandarache, and you would only have to cross a rambla and very easily, as analyzed now.

From this exit, in a straight line you reach the "Blind Tower" where the great Roman cemetery is, and follows La Aparecida and La Puebla (Una mutatio), but before in the place of La Asomada, where the base of another "blind tower" has appeared as a memory of the name, or in homage to a deceased character of a certain celebrity or wealth. It was customary to put them on the crossroads of roads or special places.

The proposal is that:

From this new "Torreciega" or funerary monument in memory of some illustrious character, or perhaps a little later, the road was diverted to Eliocroca, with four mutationis every seven miles plus two to eight miles. This route would follow a practically straight line to the place of El Paretón. Except a small curve before reaching the village of Las Palas. Whose name has a clear Latin origin.

The average slope of this section is only 2%!

(In 100 meters of road, 2 meters are climbed)

And it is quite possible that the foundation was only from a layer of gravel, since almost everything is clay soil or compacted plaster.

From La Asomada (More or less) to La Magdalena, next mutatio, the only apparently unstable ford to cross it, would be the Rambla de Benipila, but at the height of La Guía, shortly before the Paraje del Pozo de los Palos (Whose name is a total unknown, because it does not have any well).

Palus? In Latin it has two more common meanings; one is that it is a pole, wood or mannequin for the exercise of the legionaries. The other is more applicable to Cabo de Palos, as it means pond, swamp, aguazal, etc.

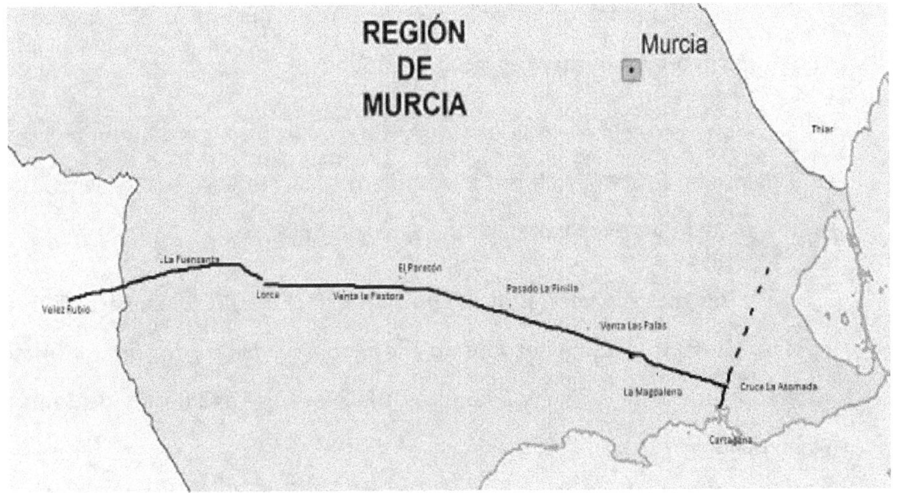

(Route from Cartagena to Lorca)

Around here, the rambla is very wide, about 50 meters, and very shallow. Of small boulders and gravel. The margins today do not exceed 80 cm in height, so it can be deduced that, two thousand years ago, the height was half.

Very easy to traverse practically all year round.

Or perhaps it would be crossed through a cheap and simple wooden bridge. That would rise very little (1.5 mt) above the level of the margins of the rambla.

And very easy to repair, if necessary. The possible storms and their floods, which affect this rambla, occur statistically every ten years on average.

The next mutatio may be located in the "Venta de las Palas", which appears on the oldest maps, and which would be located about one kilometer from the current town of Las Palas, in the direction of La Pinilla and Lorca. The reference of the distance in km, would be added to the award of "Sale" (Mutatio) that still appears today on the maps.

The mutatio of La Pinilla, would be located about 3-4 km, towards the next one that is that of the Paretón.

In El Paretón, the road makes a turn of more than 100 degrees, towards Lorca, and nearby, a miliary has also been found.

The possible mutatio of El Paretón, comes from Latin and means: dam, wall of a dam, etc. Just where there is a modern concrete wall, which dams, backwaters and regulates a little the waters of the Guadalentín River.

The route is very straight, presumably cheap in its construction, and runs parallel (O Bajo) in some sections to the modern highway to Vera, in Almeria, and where an iron mine was discovered by the place of Los Puertos de Santa Barbara, when building it.

This proposed route also completely borders the Guadalentín, on its southern side, so it seems that it is not necessary for bridges to be built. (It is a Roman-style hypothesis, very practical and low maintenance)

And from Lorca, continuing towards the source of the river, which can already be called Luchena, the road makes a slight curve, looking for Andalusia and bordering the hill, where you can see the ruins of the castle of Xiquena, and the places or flus of houses of La Fuensanta, Girona, Fontanares, etc., goes to Vélez Rubio, already in the province of Almería. Along this path two miliaries have been found that confirm this route (Against the proposal of P. Sillieres), and it is also much shorter, with water, safer and more discreet.

The exact location of the old Lorca (Whether it is called Eliocroca or another name) would be hidden north of the Peña Rubia, where the thirteenth century castle is located. And next to the Guadalentín River.

And here is one of the errors of compilation of the Itinerary:

The mystery of the mansio of Ad Morum and the lack of some other "stop" between Eliocroca (Lorca) and Basti (Baza), which is about 50 kms away.

It has already been commented on in paragraph 4.

The hypothesis, as I mentioned in <<History of the Bishopric of Cartagena>> is that, once the region and all of Hispania were ruined, by the Franks and Alamanni in 262, the roads (cursus publicus) are traced by small merchants and artisans, but without the greatness of means and objectives of the Res Pública.

This situation of hardship, and of general crisis, can give us an idea when studying the royal roads to the year 1600. And in which there is a turnaround in the "Routes" and roads, with respect to what were the Roman roads.

As an example, let's see in the section of "Rotero de España" of the work <<Epitome Cosmographico>> by the Portuguese G, by Souza, and on page 495, the way:

"From Valencia to Granada, 75 Leagues":

Cataroja--Alginete--Alcudia--alcocer—Jativa—Vallada—Mugen—La fuente la Higuera—Alcaudete—Yecla—Inmilla—La venta del indio—Calaspara—La venta de Carauaca—La venta de languera—..........

The sale of moral—The sale of Martin Serrano—Güesca---(Roman Tugi)-Baza-------------------------Granada.

If you look at a map, it is the shortest journey, in kms, from Fuente la Higuera to Baza. Almost a straight line.

Ad Morum in Latin can be translated as: "Towards the wild morality" (Blackberry). Too much agreement with the still active today, Venta del Moral. (Unbelievable)

Around 1500, it seems that the stops or old mutationis, become "Sales", as can be seen in their proliferation in all the routes of Spain, as references of the royal roads, where you could eat, sleep, etc.

La Venta del Moral, is located north of Lorca or the Ad Morum, but about 70 kms.

And with a certain "parallelism" in its route, converging in Baza (Basti). At the moment and in the absence of documents, the subject is left open to all kinds of research, and we continue to analyze this road, accepting the name of A-4, and new locations are proposed from **Acci** (Guadix) to **Castulonem** (Linares).

The **A-4**, is registered (With departure in Cartagena) in the Itinerary as:

Eliocroca	mpm LXIIII
Ad Morum	mpm XXIIII
Basti	mpmp XVI
Acci	mpm XXV
Acatucci	mpm XXVIII, 41.5 km
Viniolis	mpm XXIIII, 35.5 km.
Mentesa Bastia	mpm XX, 29,6 km.
Castulone	mpm XX, 32,5 km.

The proposal is as follows, and with the simple technique of comparing distances and applying their possible geographical difficulties. Also comparing the different proposals that appear in the Hierosolymitanum and discarding the majority, for not having any basis or documentary support.

From Acci:

Acatucci is Guadahortuna, 45km by road from Guadix

Viniolis es Jódar (Jaén), 35.5 km from Guadahortuna.

Mentesa Bastia is Ubeda, about 30 km from Jódar. And about 32.9 from the current Linares.

The total distance in Roman miles is: 28+24+20+22=94

94 x 1,481 = **139.2** km.

According to the consultation on the Internet, on current roads and passing through Jódar in Jaén, from Guadix in Granada to Linares in Jaén, there are **138 km!**

It seems too obvious, but it must be recognized, that the confirmation of these data and exact locations, requires more studies and tests.

And here we must remember that this is the straightest way, but it has another alternative, which does not return by the same route, but is called: From Linares to Malaga, and returns to Guadix to go down to Almeria and pay for the current Malaga.

This route is accepted as A-7, (Proposed by Eduardo Saavedra in the nineteenth century) and the Itinerary records it as:

<<Item a Castulone Malacam>> mpm CCXCI

Tugia   .   mpm XXXV

Fraxinum   .   mpm XVI

Hactara   .   mpm XXIIII

Acci	.	mpm XXXII
Alba	.	mpm XXXII
Urci	.	mpm XXIIII
Turanian	.	mpm XVI
Murgi	.	mpm XII
Saxetanum	.	mpm XXXVIII
Caviclum	.	mpm XVI
Menova .		mpm XXXIIII
Malacca	.	mpm XII

The total of this route, as it says in the statement of the Way, is 291 miles. Which is equivalent to **430.9** km.

By current roads, from Linares, through Guadix, Almeria, and to Malaga there are about **479** km

(In these, measures, between mansionis or current cities, there will always be a slight difference in the total kilometers, due to the continuous variations in the design, layout, bypass, etc., of the roads).

Then, there are about **50** km left, which can be about two mansions, given the mountainous nature of this area, until you reach Malaga.

The proposal is, from Castulone, Linares, to:

Tugia is Jaén. But not located on the current slope, but on the plain and on the road to the current Granada.

Fraxinum would be at the junction of La Cerradura towards Cambil. A XVI mpm, 23,7Km from Tugia.

Hactara es   Iznalloz, XXIIII mpm, 35.5 km from Fraxinum.

Acci,   Guadix, XXXII mpm, 47 km from Hactara

65

And then, let's continue analyzing this Way, from Acci to Málaka. Where new locations are proposed and an error or lagoon, of 50 km that are missing until the current Malaga.

From Acci, the mansionis are as follows, always according to the Hierosolymitanum:

Alba   mpm XXXII,   47.4 km

Urci   mpm XXIIII,   35.5 km

Turaniana   mpm XVI,   23.7 km

Murgi   mpm XII,   17.8 km

Saxetanum   mpm XXXVIII,   56.2 km

Caviclum   mpm XVI   23.7 km

Menova   mpm XXXIIII   50.3 km

Malaka   mpm XII 17.8 km

The new locations that are proposed are:

Alba   is   Abla, 41.5 km by the A-92 R2 Motorway. About 6 km less than by the Roman road, perhaps attributable to the fact that the current highway, crosses almost in a straight line all the ramblas, streams, and all the geographical features that can hinder a Roman road of more than 2000 years ago.

Urci 35.5 km from Abla, could be located, with many doubts in a place with few houses and almost abandoned inhabitants, called La Fuente Santa.

From here, the road would pass near the large and important Iberian site of Los Villares, and perhaps cross the Andarax River through Gádor, and what seems a succession of villages and small settlements that took advantage of the fresh water of the Andarax for agriculture.

Turaniana, 23.7 km away, could be Benahadux. Although it also has possibilities the very close and "Latin" Pechina. (Pendentive in Latin, means clam or mollusk shell). Almost certainly renamed Franco around 1300, but as you can see, with Latin roots.

Murgi, the current Almeria, located in some settlement or hill, in the direction of Malaga.

Saxetanum, would be the current Adra, about XXXVIII miles, (**56.2** km) that fully coincides with the road distance: **55.4** km. From Almeria.

In many places you can read that Adra is Abdera, because some reckless authors, without any document or foundation, it seems that, by simple and unfounded homonymy, they have published and propagated it.

Fortunately, Wikipedia, in its prudence, wisely puts it as "Discussion", and apart from the "daring" that has "uploaded" it to the Net, the Wiki, then, and then also, describes the Greek Abdera that already consists towards the **650!** a.C., in Macedonia, and area of the coast of Thrace. Very close to the mouth of the Nestos River. And add more data.

Analyze that, in those years, the Hispanics of Adra of the aforementioned time, would be small groups of 100-200 individuals, who did not know the wheel or the iron, and collected limpets and crabs, with some rabbit or goat from time to time. Abdera's name appears very late and is pending much study. Surely it was a mutatio.

Caviclum would come to be located near (Prope, in Latin) the town of Melicena, 23.7 from Adra.

Menova, by distance in km, is close to Almuñecar, Granada. About 50 km from Melicena. With doubts.

And finally, malaka's mansio is recorded, which could be located in Nerja. But adding Roman miles and their equivalent in kilometers, it turns out that there are about 50 km to the current and recognized Malaga.

From Almeria capital to Malaga, in mpm they add up to the equivalent of **148** km, while on current roads they are **210** km. With the normal bias of application by ring roads and several others, it seems evident that, from Almuñécar to the current Malaga, mansionis are missing. Pending study.

Paragraph 7

Libisosia, Parietinis and Saltigi

(Lezuza, Parietinis and Chinchilla?)

In the Itinerary of G. Parthey appears:

a-Libisosia, or Libisosa, is Lezuza

b-Parietinis, es Chinchilla, (Cortés) or San Clemente (Lapie) c-Saltigi or Saltici, appears in the Itinerary, associated with Jorquera (Albacete) according to Cortés and Santa María del Campo, according to Paul Lapie. (It was to refer to St. Mª del Campo Rus, in Cuenca, as there is another in Burgos)

Analysis:

As on page 352, of the Itinerary of G. Parthey, Libisosia appears as it is Lezuza, in Albacete, (According to Lapie and Cortés), because some authors go and upload it to Wikipedia, and it is published in all the tourist guides of towns and provinces, and wherever they let it be published.

It is also read in some places (especially in tourism pamphlets) that, Saltici, is Chinchilla *"Since always"*.

What meaning does it have: since always?

It would be necessary to take into account some points, so that the concepts are clear and deepen in those that do not have enough solidity, so that it has to be investigated more deeply.

The proposal is to start from several points:

1-Libisosia, Parietinis and Saltici, appear on the A-31 route,

<<Item to Laminio alio itinere Caesaraugustam>>, which as analyzed before, suffers from "gaps" and lack of data, which make it impossible to trace this route, from Laminio (Almodóvar del Campo) to Zaragoza.

2-These three mansionis, also appear and in the same order, in the Vessels of Vicarello. That as we have already seen, they register the mansionis with a denomination that only appear in the Vessels. And they only coincide with the data collected by Parthey in the ancient and original *Itinerary,* in the most important cities, such as Hispalis, Coruba, Cástulo, the three mansionis of the subject, and then jump to Valencia, from where they continue to Rome.

3-In the analysis of distances, according to the Vessels, and from front to back, we see that from Játiva (Saetabis) going back to Ad Aras, there are XXVIII miles, which are about: 41.46 km.

They coincide with the current Sales that are very close to Fuente la Higuera, at the junction to Alicante-Murcia-Andalusia, and on the other to the mountain pass of Almansa, Almansa city, Chinchilla, Albacete, etc.

Libisosa---XXII—Parietinis—XVI—Saltigi—XXXII—Ad Palem—XXII—Ad Aras

Libisosa... 32.5 km... Parietinis... 23,6km... Saltigi... 47,4km... Ad Palem... 32,5km... Ad Aras

Libisosa.   Bullet?

Parietinis   .   Near the Cathedral of Albacete.

Saltigi   .   .   Hoya Gonzalo, or nearby.

Ad Palem   .   Near Almansa. Crossing of......

Ad Aras.   Sales of Fuente la Higuera, on the highway that comes from Játiva to Almansa and Albacete.

Remember, that the technique used, is to take a reliable source of departure, as it is in this case to Játiva. Documented and beyond doubt.

Therefore, it seems that **Saltigi**, is located, or perhaps is, the same Iberian town that is in the town of Hoya Gonzalo. As some authors have pointed out, although without the same analysis or arguments, of this humble author.

The two cemeteries or necropolis, of the Iberian town of Hoya Gonzalo, indicate a large population and a slight change or adaptation of the town to new times. It is documented that around 170 BC.C., the Romans imposed on all Hispanic settlements, the abandonment of their settlements in hills and walled, and ordered that their new settlements be installed in flat and unfortified places. This implies or seems to indicate greater control of the people, by the Roman Empire. (To be investigated)

Parietinis, comes to coincide with the place where the current cathedral of Albacete is located. Coincidence?

Libisosa, it would beabout 32.5 km away, but in the direction of Cástulo, (Linares) along the current road that passes through Balazote, El Jardín, etc. (N-322)

By the National-430, the distance from the capital to Lezuza, would be around 50 km. As the crow flies: 43 km.

So, it seems proper, rule out that it is Lezuza. It is farther away and in another direction.

According to the Vessels of Vicarello, Libisosa would come from Linares on the N-322, and if it could be confirmed that Parietinis is Albacete, Libisosa would be right in **Balazote**.

Another note about the current Lezuza is that its old name is unknown and it was almost certainly renamed during the so-called Reconquista, around 1240, by the Christian armies and their Frankish collaborators.

Its name comes from the village of Le Zouze, in Marseille, where La Zouze television, La Zouze dance and theater school, etc. are also recorded. And logically it is Castilianized when put in writing, such as: Lezuza. (The ou in French reads as u)

Zouz is also a surname in France.

Like Munuera, a town near Lezuza, it is also a surname and has its origin in the French Munere.

(See the book: <<*Male France and Grandma Germany. Origin of place names, surnames and more from all over Spain and Portugal*>>, great work.)

About Balazote and his possible graces or merits, almost nothing can be said in documentary form. The most important thing is that it is on the road that connects Linares with Albacete, and from it to Valencia and Rome. Or to Complutum and Carthago Nova.

And we must remember that, around 90% of the great communication routes of Spain and Portugal, coincide with the Roman roads.

Another possible endorsement of Balazote, can be, his Bicha, sculpture found very close to the town, and although it has a somewhat mysterious origin, between Iberian, Greek, or anabolic, it is a point in its favor, to constitute the mansio Libisosia or Libisosa.

Balazote, also has a Frankish origin, in the surname Balazot, with origin in Burgundy, department of Nievre.

(Forget what Wikipedia says about it)

4-About Chinchilla de Montearagón, it must be said that Chinchilla is a name and a surname of French origin.

Montearagón also has a French origin. It is also a villa in Huesca and other places. The place where the current Chinchilla is now located, of unknown name or not located with certainty, would be renamed by the Christian conquerors and their French collaborators, around 1242.

It can be said that everything that begins with Mont-, has a frank origin.

Like so many other towns in the area, such as: Caudet-e, Bonet-e, Almanza and Almansa, La Roda, San Clement-e, Albacet-e, Hellin-e, Agramon-t, Tobarr-e, Sisant-e, Muner-a, etc., etc.

Any application or temptation of homonymy, or phonetic resemblance, must be discarded beforehand. Since the place names are happening over the years and centuries, as the different merchants, invaders or colonizers arrive. And they are renaming them.

Not forgetting the mistakes of the *"Public Scriwamen"* and geographers. That they are numerous, and although they are slight, they induce to misinterpret the locations.

(See section 14, on ancient and modern authors)

Thus, the Phoenicians begin to register names and places, for the control of their commercial interests. Like the Thader River in Murcia (Rio Segura), or the Thiar mansio, between Elche and Cartagena in the Campoamor area, etc.

On the other hand, any reference to "pre-Roman" names must be treated with great caution or almost better forgotten. Hispanics had no recognized writing, so it would be normal for oral tradition to be lost. The Greeks are the first to create a Greek-Iberian script, in the Levant area, around the third century. Its center seems to be Elche and its port in Santa Pola, and going up the Vinalopó Valley to Caudete, Almansa and surroundings. Including the Murcian part of Mula, Caravaca, etc. And from the East to Alcoy. (Where lead plates with writing have been found" Greek ibera")

The Romans record it all in Latin.

It seems that Hispanics did not name their towns. Or they have not reached us, because they had no writing. They are the Romans, the great organizers.

Paragraph 8

The *Hierosolymitanum Itinerary* awards, numerous locations, although without an explanatory basis.

As they have beeneaten before, it is not G's fault. Parthey the author of the Hierosolymitanum, if not, which, as they say today:

"The company is not responsible for the opinions of the tertulianos"

And these tertulianos or authors who appear in the Itinerary H. in Hispania, are:

Conrad Mannert, German (1756-1834), historian and geographer. Personally, I hold him in esteem, because apart from considering him the most prudent, in terms of his assessments and opinions, he marked the location of the mansio Esuri, in Castro Marim, Portugal.

Paul Lapie, French, who came very high in France, but his proposals for localization in Hispania, are somewhat weak.

Valckenaer, Charles Athanase (1771–1852) Born in Paris, he studied at Oxford and Glasgow. Engineer, entomologist, politician, poet, mayor of Paris, geographer, etc., etc.

It seems that he touched on too many topics, to be an expert in any. He also dared with the Roman roads, and the locations of some Roman cities. Immense and almost unfathomable themes.

Graberg di Hemsö, was a Swede born in 1776, very adventurous and military under the orders of the British Empire. In the end he stayed in Italy and stood out as a "marine geographer".

Reichard, another German. Perhaps he lacks depth in his assessments.

Miguel Cortés y López, (1777-1854) canon, polygraph, politician and Aragonese historian, academician of the Royal Academy of History.

His biography seems to be traced from that of Valckenaer. They were even born the same year and almost died the same. But Michael was a refugee in France and in addition to being a political linguist, geographer, etc., he worked as a priest, so it seems somewhat adventurous or reckless.

Sestini, etc.

75

Paragraph 9

The A-23 Road

<<Item ab Ostio fluminis Anae Emerita>>

This route can be the example of the tremendous practicality of the engineers of the Roman Empire, which was discussed above, in its application to the crossings of rivers and ramblas, and the saving of its inevitable construction of bridges.

And by the way, locations of old mansionis are proposed, although only the stretch from Ostio to the Roman *Itálica*, today in the Sevillian Santiponce, on the other side of the Guadalquivir River and Hispalis, Seville.

The missing stretch from Itálica to Emerita Augusta will be seen later.

1.Ostio—XXIIII—2. Praesidio—XXVIII—3. Ad Rubras—XXVIII-- 4. Onoba--XXX—5. Ilipa—XXII--6. Tucci --XVI—7. Italic.

Its equivalent is the following proposals and current locations:

1.Albufeira (Portugal)—35.5km—2. **Faro** (Portugal)—41,46km—3. **Ayamonte** (Spain)... —4. Onoba--41.46 km--5. Ilipa--44.43 km—6 Tucci--26km--7. **Santiponce**

(Another big issue is, how was the bridge or passage of the Guadiana from Spain to Portugal. Possibly it was from boats or pontoons. As it appears carved on the column of Trajan, in Rome, crossing the Danube River. They are also famous for enduring until the eighteenth and nineteenth centuries, in Seville and in Cádiz, where there were three.)

Onoba would be near the current Gibraleón, north of Huelva capital.

Tucci, would be near Benacazón, or Sanlúcar la Mayor.

Ilipa, around Bonares.

Itálica, in Santiponce, was created in 206 BC.C., as a prize to retire many legionaries. But on the other side of the Guadalquivir, in the old area of present-day Seville, Híspalis a mysterious, or unknown, population begins to grow and becomes large and important around 45 b.C. with the favors of Julius Caesar and his administration.

As Híspalis grows, the ancient Itálica is losing importance.

Itálica is on the right of the Guadalquivir and Híspalis on the left. (Always in the direction of its mouth and the sea)

The Via and the mansionis, which register the Vessels of Vicarello, from Cádiz to Rome, are located in the south of the Guadalquivir, through Seville, Córdoba, etc., and cross it in its upper part, more or less by Linares, in the direction of Albacete and Fuente la Higuera in Valencia.

Paragraph 10

Analysis of the A-14 Route

<<Item ab Olisipone Emeritam>>

Location of Badajoz, Évora, Lisbon, and others.

This route from Lisbon to Merida, seems to be the first or the most popular, but it should be noted, that it has two more *"alio itinere"* others, that is, two more alternative roads. The A-16 and the A-17.

The first proposal is as follows:

The ancient Olisipone, would come to be or be located in the small port of Montijo, southeast of the current and immense Lisbon, since it is facing Mérida, on the left bank of the river and saving the great estuary of the Tagus River (Tejo in Portuguese) and the extensive marshes or lowlands, so difficult and unhealthy for humans.

This A-14 documents a total of 161 Roman miles (mpm), which is equivalent to about 238 km.

Given the difficulty of the analysis to try to recognize the possible route of this road, the proposal goes through leaving Mérida on its northern side and saving the Guadiana River, and reaching La Puebla de la Calzada, Valdelacalzada, and reaching Gévora about 50 km and possible mansio called *Ad Adrum flumen* (Towards the Adro River)

This mansio is located about six kilometers north of the city of Badajoz and on the other side of the Guadiana River.

Let us also remember that the Roman roads had a clear sense of military use, and their proximity to towns, colonies, civitas, etc., were an added bonus to their use.

Let's now look at the relationship of mansionis:

Olisipone – Emeritam	*mpm CLXI,238 km.*
Equabona . . .	mpm XII, 17.77 km
Catobriga . . .	mpm XII, 17.77 km

Caecilian	.	.	.	mpm VIII, 11.8 km
Malececa	.	.	.	mpm XXVI, 38.5 km
Salacia	.	.	.	mpm XII, 17.77 km
Ebora	.	.	.	mpm XLIIII, 65 km
Ad Adrum flumen		.	.	mpm VIIII, 13.3 km
Dipone	.	.	.	mpm XII, 17.77 km
Evandriana	.	.	.	mpm XVII, 25 km
Emerita	.	.	.	mpm VIIII, 13.3 km

The distances from Montijo, on the other side of the Tagus River and Lisbon, to Merida, coincide fully in kilometers, along the old road with the distance in Roman miles. (mpm)

So, the localization proposals are the following:

Olisipone is Montijo, on the left bank of the Tagus. The current Lisbon is on the right bank of the river. (Always looking at the ocean)

Catobriga, would be located in the town of Pegoes, on the N-114.

Caeciliana, around the current Vendas Novas, N-114.

Salacia, seems to be the current **Evora!**

Ebora, would be 65 km from the previous one, and would be Elvas, still in Portugal.

Ad Adrum flumen, is Gévora, located to the north and six km from Badajoz capital.

Like Ilici (Elche), Numancia (Soria), Eliocroca (Lorca), Chinchilla? and others, the Muslims moved the ancient Roman settlements to higher places with better defense.

Dipone and Evandriana, it is not known, but it can be said that the current Puebla de la Calzada is a mutatio. For Puebla, and for Calzada.

Several villages in the surrounding area carry the apostillo of "Calzada", which can be a good historical or popular reference. Although perhaps relative or of little entity.

Paragraph 11

The A-22 a route, and the A-22b, some proposals.

The A-22 b Route

<<Item ab Esuri per compendium Pace Iulia>>

mpm LXXVI, (112.5 km)

Esuri is Castro Marim

Pace iulia is Castelo Branco

Linking this topic with the previous section, some daring proposals will be made, although with full awareness, that they can be very relative, and that their foundations, whether limited or not have a good basis, since a great doubt arises with the mysterious path of the A-22 b, and its correct or adequate translation of the Latin phrase: "per compendium". And its very short distance. (Which may be a mistake.)

The basis for the study of this A-22 a, are the mansionis of: Salacia and Eboram, which are on the route of the A-14, analyzed in the previous section. They are recorded in the same direction as the A-22 a, from Esuri to Pace iulia.

Due to the distance that the miles in the header add up, the 395 km, and the location in the middle of the layout of the mansionis Salacia and Eboram, it can be formulated that the route that begins in Esuri is the current **Castro Marim** on the right bank of the Guadiana, in front of the Spanish Ayamonte.

From Castro Marim it goes up to Beja, then passes and uses two common mansionis of the A-14, Evora and Elvas (Salaria and Ebora) and continues north to **Castelo Branco**, where Pace iulia would be located.

This stretch of road along the current and old roads (Saving the highways) adds up to a total of 390 km, five less than the totals announced by the original in Latin in miles, **395.**

Due to the distances, it seems that everything coincides, but in the absence of data, it is considered only a proposal. It remains pending a lot of research and study. That is already in process and of prompt publication.

The A-22 b, is a mystery, and does not agree in distance. Either it is one of the several errors that the I. Hierosolymitanum collects in the distances or much research work remains.

<<Item ab Esuri per compendiun Pace iulia>>	mpm LXXVI sic
Myrtili	mpm XL
Pace iulia	mpm XXXVI

These 76 Roman miles of the route, equivalent to about **112.5 km**, while, by the "normal" road, they mark a total of **395 km**.

This relationship between one distance and another is too broad to be reasonable and logical. It seems to be a mistake.

As a curiosity, the 112.5 km, coincide with the distance from Castro Marim to Beja (115 km)

It may be a coincidence, but given the mistakes that have been made in the Hispanic Vías analyzed by this author, which are not all, it is very likely to have foundation. Since, on the less important roads, moregaps and errors are demonstrated in the records.

Paragraph 12

The A-1 and A-2

From the Pyrenees to Tarragona and its detours to Zaragoza and Cartagena.

(Some differences)

83

According to the Itinerarium Antonini Augusti Et Hierosolymitanum, which compiles and orders in some way, the different documentary sources on the Roads or roads of the entire Roman Empire, the study of those called in Hispania as the A-1 and the A-2, show very clearly some differences, which support my hypothesis, about the great influence caused by the invasions of Franks and Alamanni in the year 262.

(We again show the admiration for Gustav Parthey as author and Moritz Pinder as editor, of the Hierosolymitanum)

At the same time, they serve as an imperishable documentary source, to study and locate some mansionis, also mutationis, and to try to understand a little more history in general, and the innumerable advances of Roman engineers.

The so-called A-1, is supposed to be the first Roman road that enters Hispania, (although it seems that it has a background in Carthaginian and Iberian engineering) and does so through the Pyrenees of Girona.

From the French Ad Stabulum, the current **Le Boulou**, it reaches Ad Pyreneum which is located in: **La junquera,** Girona, XVI miles away.

The mansionis of the **A-1**, according to Itinerary A. A. Hierosolymitanum are:

Ad Pyreneum	mpm XVI	**La Junquera**
Iuncaria	mpm XVI	**Figueras**
Gerunda	mpm XXVII	**Girona**
Barcenonempm LXVI		**Barcelona**
Stabulo Novompm LI		**¿?**
Tarracone	mpm XXIIII	**Tarragona**

It continues through Lleida to Zaragoza and ends in León.

But in the cold or mechanical relationship of the same Itinerary, in the next route, the **A-2,** and in the theoretical same relationship of mansionis, the following appear:

Ruscione**	mpm
Ad Centurions**	mpm XX
Summo Pyreneo**	mpm V
Iuncaria	mpm XVI
Cinniana	mpm XV
Aquis Voconis	mpm XXIIII
Seterras	mpm XV
Praetorio	mpm XV
Barcenone	mpm XVII
Purposes**	mpm XX
Antistian**	mpm XVII
Palfuriana**	mpm XIII
Tarracone	mpm XVII

As you can see, the stations with double asterisk, do not appear on the A-1 road.

Reason?

Also missing is Gerunda, Girona.

They are only assumptions, but the causes of these gaps and changes in the names of the mansionis, support the theory of the invasions of Franks and Alamanni.

This area of France and Gaul in general, like Hispania, had long been at peace and absent of conflicts. The vigilant legionaries and their chiefs, must have been plump and physically lacking, so Pax, and did not endure for long the force of the invaders.

For the brute and brave "tourists" who came from Germany, (Franks and Alamanni) the invasion of Mediterranean France had to be a triumphant walk, although its devastation was at the height of the worst. When entering Hispania, it seems normal, that they follow the path marked by the comfortable roads, and raze or destroy all the mansionis and mutationis that seemed to them. At the same time as towns, cities and so on. Elche among them.

And to roll it a little more, in the theme of the changing mansionis, although at the same time it also documents it, the "Stops" or Sales of the Vicarello Glasses appear. Where they appear:

Ruscinonem   mpm (In France)

In Pyrineum   mpm XVI

Iuncaria   mpm XV

Cilnianam   mpm XII

Gerundam   mpm XII

Aquis Vocontis   mpm XV

Seterras   mpm XXIIII

Semproniana   mpm VIIII

Arragonem   mpm XX

Ad Fines   mpm XVII

Antistianam   mpm XIII

Palfuriana   mpm XVI

Tarracone   mpm XXV

Here in this relationship, it is immediately noticeable that it is missing: Barcelona.

The study is open to investigation.

Summary of the A-2 and its comparison with the Vicarello Vessels:

Itinerary A. A. et H..			*Vicarello glasses*		
Narbone	.	.	.	Narbonem	
Ad Vicensium	.	XX	.	.	.
Combusta	.	XIIII	.	Combusta	.	XXXII
Ruscione	.	VI	.	Ruscinonem	.	SAW
Ad Centurions	.	XX	.	.	.	.
Summo Pyreneo .		V	.	In Pyraeneum	.	XXV
Iuncaria	.	XVI	.	Iuncaria	.	XV
Cinniana	.	XV	.	Cilniana	.	XII
Here Voconis	.	XXIIII	.	Gerundam	.	XII
Seterras	.	XV	.	Here Vocontis	

Praetorio	.	XV	.	Seterras
Barcenone	.		.	Semproniana
Purposes		.	.	Arragonem
Antistian	.	.	.	Ad Fines
Palfuriana	.	.	.	Antistian
Tarracone	.	.	.	Palfurianam
.	.	.	.	.	Tarracone

The errors or errata, start from Narbone to Combusta, which in the Itinerary add up to 20 plus 14, which are: 34.

While in the Vessels, they add up to 32 miles. And the mansio of Ad Vicensium is missing.

In the Itinerary, Gerundam is missing.

In the Vessels, Barcenone does not appear, and a "new" one does appear: Semproniana.

Dare the reader to find his own conclusions.

On the A-1 road, between Barcenone and Tarracone there is only one mansio: Stabulo Novo, while in the Vessels there are four, whose sum of three of them, is the distance from Barcelona to Tarragona.

But this route is already done in a straight line and not passing through the sea port of Barcelona.

The Franks and Alamanni seem to have erased the port and population of Barcenone, but once the destruction of the invaders has passed, the former users of the road have opened or discovered and used a shorter and rectilinear road.

It's just a theory.

Paragraph 13

From Tarracone to Valentia

According to the Hierosolymitanum Itinerary:

Mansionis	*mpm*	*Location proposal*
Tarracone		Tarragona
Oleastrum	XXI	Hospitalet del Infante
Traia Capita	XXIIII	La Ampolla
Dertosa	XVII	Tortosa
Intibili	XXXVII	San Mateu
Ildun	XXIIII	La Puebla Tornesa
Sepelaci	XXIIII	Near Burriana
Saguntum	XXII	Sagunto
(Puebla de Farnals	VIII, a mutatio)	
Valentia	XVI	Valencia

Moving the mpm or Roman miles to kilometers, the distances fully agree.

Now, the exact situation of some mansionis is a more delicate issue and more pending of the new findings, and of the work of archaeologists and other scientific disciplines, and of the depth of their works.

The mansionis that appear in the Vessels, change a little, for example:

Near Sagunto, Sepelaci disappears, and Ad Noulas appears with two more miles. That then compensates, subtracting two to the next one towards Tarragona, Ildun.

Between Tarragona and Tortosa, the mansionis of Oleastrum and Traia Capita disappear and are replaced (In the Vessels) by that of Sub Saltum.

The conclusion of this could be: that some names or place names that refer to specific places or towns disappear, and instead the much more generic and ambiguous ones appear, such as Ad Noulas (Towards the noulas) or Sub Saltum, (Towards the gorge). In free translation.

Paragraph 14

Importance of ancient, modern and contemporary authors.

This is a very delicate message and chapter, in that it can hurt sensibilities, but it is necessary for everything to be documented, and it is stressed again, and advises on prudence and humility when launching categorical sentences, without sufficient documentary basis.

For this author, the paradigmatic example is the German researcher. But beware, without contempt of the great American researchers, the discreet English, the great Swiss discoverer of Petra, the French, etc.

Let no one feel offended, but when reading and analyzing the Itinerary A. A. et Hierosolymitanum, the phrase appears in a possible location of a mansio or city:

"Prope"

(Latin means: "Near")

It can already be deduced, that it almost certainly comes from some German researcher. And all will not be perfect, it is clear, but they seem the example to follow in this research of History and its few signs or indications.

Practically, they are the only ones who use the "Prope" of Latin, which was the language in which nineteenth-century researchers understood each other.

They preferred not to sin and say locations without a good basis, and their opinion, in the absence of confirmation or doubts, was to put "Close to"

And in the opposite part, although without saying names, appears a Spanish of the nineteenth century, and following the same trail some of the twentieth, which deduces and affirms in this singular way:

"Because from Consaburum, Consagurum comes and from here Consuegra.

Just like grandfather you get to "agüelo" and from good to "güeno"

And in another boast, it applies the one that:

"Moose means palace in Greek, so it is Alcazar de San Juan"

And that Tudemir is Murcia capital, for: "Several reasons". (You have to read it to believe it)

And the worst thing is that, The Hierosolymitanum, and the errors it contains in the studies and relationship of authors, has expanded its fantastic and erroneous load, in the style of the philosophical current of the sophists in ancient Greece throughout Europe and the world.

(Sophism used some truths to arrive at a general lie, or deception. Basically.)

A personal study, of the successes of the several authors that appear in the aforementioned Itinerary, and remembering that it is from the nineteenth century, appears to us as a percentage, which is approximately 15%.

50% of the places proposed are unverifiable, at the moment, due to the lack of reliable documents, small indications, etc., and about 35%, is of a clamorous error, or documentary recklessness. Or pretentious interest.

The question seems to be, the one that has been chaining the ambiguous information of the Phoenician and Greek authors, with the very worked and recorded, although very partial of the Roman that has reached us until today.

The great leap, from the year 400 to 1000, (Approx.) is something like a documentary debacle, and then lasts until 1450, when technical advances are reflected in much more complete and advanced maps (Tabulas).

But at the level of the Roman roads, the great authors of maps, collect the few documents that remain, which are practically the same as those we have today.

And the errors or inaccuracies are also transmitted until today.

And at this point, we must comment on the importance of the ancient maps of the sixteenth and seventeenth century, where Nicolas Sanson, Mercator, Ortelius, etc., contribute their knowledge about the Roman roads and their mansionis, but suffering from a certain documentary audacity, by placing them in the primitive maps, but more by intuition than by documentation, and lacking, above all, of the great information and studies that we have today.

But beware, that "certain documentary daring" is sometimes very positive to find solutions to some problems and geographical or historical gaps.

Nor is the great contribution of these makers of Tabulas or maps, where they reflected in the knowledge that was available, at that time, the documents of the Roman Empire, diminished or undervalued.

In summary, all the work of these geographers cited is very positive, their maps are very advanced and meticulous, but you have to look with a magnifying glass at the Roman roads and roads they cite, because they are ambiguous and imprecise in some cases or in part of some routes.

Index

And then follow the road to Guadix (Acci), go up to Linares.

(Castulo) by the first route and returns through Jaén capital, to

Guadix, by another route different from the first. Arrive in Almeria

Bibliography

It is just a sample of the numerous consultations that can and should be made, just to get a little closer to the subject of Roman roads.

--Anonymous of Ravenna (Called, The Ravenate)

(Hispania: Chapters 42 to 45 of Book IV and 3-4 of Book V.)

--Bibliogaraphic Records of the Ancient World

--Castilia Veteris nova descriptio (Mercator)

--Diccionario Geográfico-Histórico de la España Antigua, Tarraconense, Bética y Lusitana (Miguel Cortés y López)

--Digital Atlas of Roman Empire. (Lund University, Sweden)

--Digital Maps Roman Empire.

--Cosmographic Epitome where all the cities of the world appear.   (Gabriel de Sousa Brito)

--Sacred Spain; Geographical and Historical Theatre of the Church
          (Henriquez Florez)

--Geneanet

--History of the Bishopric of Cartagena. From Antiquity to the Thirteenth Century.

          (Ando-Enmanuel Gall)

--Natural History (Pliny the Elder)

--Hispania veteris descriptio (1590, Parergon)

--Itinerarium Antonini Augusti Et Hierosolymitanum

          (Gustav Parthey, Moritz Pinder)

--Mother France and Grandma Germany. Origin of surnames and place names throughout Spain and Portugal.

(Ando-Enmanuel Gall)

--Liste des voies romaines. (Wikipedia)

--Map of the bishopric of Toledo

--Map of the bishopric and kingdom of Murcia (Thomas López, 1768)

--Repertoire of all the roads of Spain. (Peter John Villuga)

--Tabula moderna Hispaniae (Sebastian Munster, 1540)

--Utriusque Castiliae Nova descriptio (Joan Blaeu, 1635)

--Wikipedia

Etc.

Etc.

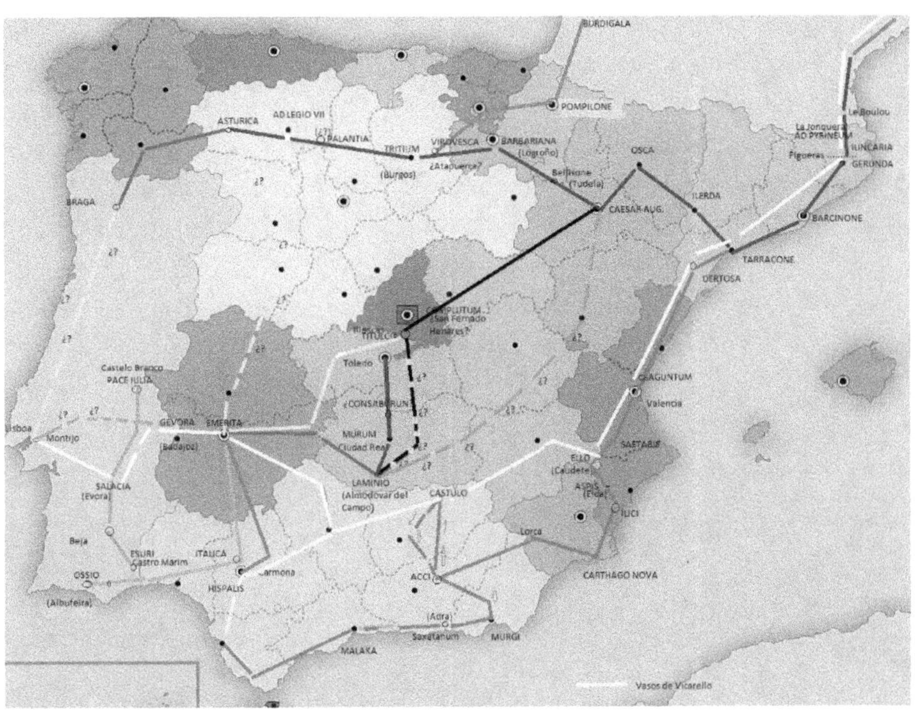

BURDIGALA
Le Boulou
La Jonquera
AD PYRINEUM
ILUNCARIA
POMPILONE
Figueras
GERUNDA
ASTURICA
AD LEGIO VII
¿F?
PALANTIA
VIROVESCA
BARBARIANA
(Logroño)
OSCA
BARCINONE
TRITIUM
¿Atapuerca?
(Burgos)
Belisone
(Tudela)
ILERDA
BRAGA
CAESAR-AUG.
TARRACONE
DERTOSA
¿F?
¿F?
¿F?
PUTUM
¿San Fernado
Henares?
¿F?
Titulcia
Toledo
SAGUNTUM
Castelo Branco
PACE IULIA
¿CONSABRUN
¿F?
Valencia
¿F?
SAETABIS
MURUM
Ciudad Real
¿F?
¿F?
ELLO
(Caudete)
Lisboa
GEVORA
EMERITA
LAMINIO
(Almodóvar del
Campo)
CASTULO
ASPIS
(Elda)
Montijo
(Badajoz)
ILICI
SALACIA
(Évora)
Lorca
CARTHAGO NOVA
Beja
ESURI
Castro Marim
ITALICA
Carmona
ACCI
OSSIO
(Albufeira)
HISPALIS
(Adra)
MURGI
Saxetanum
MALAKA
Vasos de Vicarello

This author also apologizes to them, because he also makes mistakes.

andoenmanuelgall@gmail.com